FIRST THINGS FIRST
EVERY DAY

*Because Where You're
Headed Is More Important than
How Fast You're Going*

STEPHEN R. COVEY,
A. ROGER MERRILL,
REBECCA R. MERRILL

A FIRESIDE BOOK
Published by Simon & Schuster

FIRESIDE
Rockefeller Center
1230 Avenue of the Americas
New York, NY 10020

Copyright © 1997 by Covey Leadership Center, Inc.
All rights reserved,
including the right of reproduction
in whole or in part in any form.

FIRESIDE and colophon are registered trademarks
of Simon & Schuster Inc.

Designed by Irving Perkins Associates, Inc.

Manufactured in the United States of America

1   3   5   7   9   10   8   6   4   2

Library of Congress Cataloging-in-Publication Data
Covey, Stephen R.
First things first every day : because where you're headed is
more important than how fast you're going / Stephen R.
Covey, A. Roger Merrill, Rebecca R. Merrill.
p.   cm.
"A Fireside book."
Companion volume to First things first.
1. Conduct of life.   2. Time management.   I. Merrill, A.
Roger.   II. Merrill, Rebecca R.   III. Title.
BJ1581.2.C66   1997
158.1—dc21   97-9970
CIP

ISBN 0-684-84240-8

Covey Leadership Center, Principle-Centered Leadership, The
Seven Habits of Highly Effective People, Principle-Centered Living, First Things First, Quadrant II Time Management, and *Execu-
tive Excellence* are registered trademarks of Covey Leadership Center.

Foreword
Why This Book?

Several years ago a friend shared this experience from his youth:

An old man was asked to teach a group of unruly teenage boys, including this friend, in a community program. The man was so old and the boys so "energetic" that many eyebrows were raised at the arrangement.

The first day, the old man stood at the door of the classroom and quietly handed each boy a little card as he walked in. During the class, he simply had each boy read aloud the thought that was written on the card. Then he told each boy to keep the card and to memorize the thought on it, or else they would not be able to get in the class next week.

The following week, the old man was waiting at the classroom door. Those who could not quote the thought were instructed to go and tell their parents that they would not be allowed in class. In those days this was not a desirable thing for a boy to do. So, when they hesitated, the old man offered to help them learn it "this time."

This ritual continued week after week. The friend who related this story said that after a few weeks, those little thoughts changed the whole feeling of the group. They eventually changed the course of his life. They gave him inspiration and hope years later in a foxhole far from home, and on many other challenging occasions throughout his life.

That was over forty years ago, and he still collects quotes.

Since life is busy and full of change, keeping "first things first" is a constant challenge. And maintaining focus and regaining vision is a constant need. Our hearts and minds, like all living things, need nourishment. Yesterday's meal will not satisfy today's hunger. It is regular input that provides energy and health.

So it is our hope that these little "thought bytes" will provide some daily nourishment and will be helpful to you in three ways:

1) *These "little" things will bring back the big things.*

The beach has a wonderful smell after you've been away from it for a while. A little whiff of the ocean air can bring back a flood of memories, feelings, and experiences. In the same way, a word or a phrase can often trigger the memory and understanding of a big idea and all the insight that accompanied learning it. These little thoughts will reconnect you to any positive feelings and learnings you had as you read or listened to *First Things First.*

2) *They will increase the space between stimulus and response.*

Between what happens to us and our response to it is a space. And in that space is wisdom, awareness, reflection—our inner compass. Hopefully, a quick thought byte from this little volume can create the moment it takes to visit that space and get your bearings. And the faster you're traveling, the more important that is.

3) *They will lead to and garnish your wisdom literature habit.*

Of the many responses we've received from those who have read or listened to *First Things First,* probably none has been more frequent than expressions of appreciation for the idea of the daily reading of "wisdom literature." This one practice has a profound effect on the quality of the decisions we make every day. It connects us to the principles that govern in all of life. It keeps us from being swept away by "urgency"; it keeps us focused on "importance." It helps us to stop in that space between what happens to us and our response to it and to choose a better response.

We become what we think. As James Allen so beautifully put it:

Foreword

Mind is the masterpower that molds and makes
Man is mind and evermore he takes
The tools of thought and shaping what he will
brings to pass a thousand joys and a thousand ills
He thinks in secret, it comes to pass
Environment is but his looking glass.

And as Hawthorne has said, "he who lives long in the presence of an ideal at least becomes like it." As you nourish your mind and heart on a regular basis with those things that uplift and inspire, your very nature, your character will change. And the quality of the decisions you make will be significantly enhanced. Hopefully, this book will provide a little of that nourishment, and will encourage you to make the reading of wisdom literature an important habit of your daily life.

Now, this little book will take very little room—in the office, in your purse or briefcase, at home, or in the bathroom. And it will only take a moment to read a thought or two. But, hopefully, that moment will enable you to connect with principles that have been a part of the wisdom of every truly successful individual and civilization throughout time.

As you travel through life, it's our desire that these little thoughts will become "trail markers" to help you along the way.

January 1

Basing our happiness on our ability to control everything is futile. While we do control our choice of action, we cannot control the consequences of our choices. Universal laws or principles do. Thus, *we* are not in control of our lives; *principles* are.

p.12*

* All page references are to *First Things First*.

January 2

We live in a modern society that loves short-cut techniques. Yet quality of life cannot be achieved by taking the right shortcut. There is no shortcut. But there is a path. The path is based on principles revered throughout history. If there is one message to glean from this wisdom, it is that a meaningful life is not a matter of speed or efficiency. It's much more a matter of what you do and why you do it than how fast you get it done.

p.12

January 3

The power is in the principles.

p.14

Be governed by your internal compass, not by some clock on the wall.

p.16

If the thing you've committed to do is principle-centered, you gradually become a little more principle-centered. You keep the promise to yourself and your own integrity account goes up. One of the best ways to strengthen our independent will is to make and keep promises. Each time we do, we make deposits in our Personal Integrity Account. This is a metaphor that describes the amount of trust we have in ourselves, in our ability to walk our talk. It's important to start small.

p.68

January 6

For most of us, the issue is not between the "good" and the "bad," but between the "good" and the "best." So often, the enemy of the best is the good.

p.18

January 7

In the absence of "wake-up calls," many of us never really confront the critical issues of life. Instead of looking for deep chronic causes, we look for quick-fix Band-Aids and aspirin to treat the acute pain. Fortified by temporary relief, we get busier and busier doing "good" things and never even stop to ask ourselves if what we're doing really matters most.

p.21

Paradigms are like maps. They're not the territory; they describe the territory. And if the map is wrong—if we're trying to get to someplace in Detroit and all we have is a map of Chicago—it's going to be very difficult for us to get where we want to go. We can work on our behavior—we can travel more efficiently, get a different car with better gas mileage, increase our speed— but we're only going to wind up in the wrong place fast. We can work on our attitude—we can get so "psyched up" about trying to get there that we don't even care that we're in the wrong place. But the problem really has nothing to do with attitude or behavior. The problem is that we have the wrong map.

p.25

January 9

Our problem, as one put it, "is to get at the wisdom we already have."

p.73

We're not in control; *principles* are. We can control our choices, but we can't control the consequences of those choices. When we pick up one end of the stick, we pick up the other.

p.25

While you can be efficient with things, you can't be efficient—effectively—with people.

p.26

January 12

The way we see (our paradigm) leads to what we do (our attitudes and behaviors), and what we do leads to the results we get in our lives. So if we want to create significant change in the results, we can't just change attitudes and behaviors, methods or techniques; we have to change the basic paradigms out of which they grow.

p.28

January 13

One thing's for sure: If we keep doing what we're doing, we're going to keep getting what we're getting.

p.30

January 14

We need to move beyond time management to life leadership.

p.31

It's important to realize that urgency itself is not the problem. The problem is that when urgency is the *dominant factor* in our lives, importance isn't. What we regard as "first things" are urgent things. We're so caught up in doing, we don't even stop to ask if what we're doing really needs to be done.

p.36

January 16

While management is problem-oriented, leadership is opportunity-oriented.

p.48

Values will *not* bring quality-of-life results . . . *unless we value principles.*

p.52

All the wishing and even all the work in the world, if it's not based on valid principles, will not produce quality-of-life results. It's not enough to dream. It's not enough to try. It's not enough to set goals or climb ladders. It's not enough to value. The effort has to be based on practical realities that produce the result.

p.52

The power of principles is that they're universal, timeless truths. If we understand and live our lives based on principles, we can quickly adapt; we can apply them anywhere.

p.53

To understand the application may be to meet the challenge of the moment, but to understand the principle is to meet the challenge of the moment more effectively and to be empowered to meet a thousand challenges of the future as well.

p.53

The problems in life come when we're sowing one thing and expecting to reap something entirely different.

p.56

Trust grows out of trustworthiness, out of the character to make and keep commitments, to share resources, to be caring and responsible, to belong, to love unconditionally.

p.57

Quality of life is inside-out. Meaning is in contribution, in living for something higher than self.

p.58

Between stimulus and response, there is a space. In that space is our power to choose our response. In our response lies our growth and our freedom.

p.59

January 25

Stand apart from your dreams. Look at them. Write about them. Wrestle with them until you're convinced they're based on principles that will bring results. Then use your creative imagination to explore new applications, new ways of doing things that have the principle-based power to translate dreaming to doing.

p.64

To hear conscience clearly often requires us to be "still" or "reflective" or "meditative"—a condition we rarely choose or find.

p.65

Make and keep a promise—even if it means you're going to get up in the morning a little earlier and exercise. Be sure you don't violate that commitment and be sure you don't overpromise and underdeliver. Build slowly until your sense of honor becomes greater than your moods. Little by little, your faith in yourself will increase.

p.68

January 28

Our lives are the results of our choices. To blame and accuse other people, the environment, or other extrinsic factors is to choose to empower those things to control us.

p.70

January 29

We choose—either to live our lives or to let others live them for us.

p. 70

January 30

The best way to predict your future is to create it.

p.72

If a goal isn't connected to a deep "why," it may be good, but it usually isn't best.

p.142

With the humility that comes from being principle-centered, we're empowered to learn from the past, have hope for the future, and act with confidence in the present.

p.73

Doing more things faster is no substitute
for doing the right things.

p. 73

The power to create quality of life is not in any planner. The power to create quality of life is within us—in our ability to develop and use our own inner compass so that we can act with integrity in the moment of choice.

p.73

The key to quality of life is in the compass—it's in the choices we make every day.

p.76

Where there's no gardener, there's no garden.

p.77

The more involved you are, the more significant your learning will be.

p. 78

What does it matter how much we do if what we're doing isn't what matters most?

p.89

Life is not the automatic incarnation of a planning page, no matter how well that page is written. To ignore the unexpected (even if it were possible) would be to live without opportunity, spontaneity, and the rich moments of which "life" is made.

p.93

Keep connected with your inner compass so that you can act with integrity to what's important—not necessarily to your schedule.

p.95

Quadrant II is not a tool; it's a way of thinking.

p.101

The greatest value of the process is not what it does to your schedule, but what it does to your head.

p.102

It's easy to say "no!" when there's a deeper "yes!" burning inside.

p.103

Vision is the best manifestation of creative imagination and the primary motivation of human action. It's the ability to see beyond our present reality, to create, to invent what does not yet exist, to become what we not yet are. It gives us capacity to live out of our imagination instead of our memory.

p.103

February 14

More than any other factor, vision affects the choices we make and the way we spend our time.

p.104

February 15

Conscience not only puts us in touch with our own uniqueness, it also connects us with the universal true-north principles that create quality of life.

p.111

February 16

As we learn to think win-win, we seek mutual benefit in all our interactions. We start thinking in terms of other people, of society as a whole. It profoundly affects what we see as "important," how we spend our time, our response in the moment of choice, and the results we get in our lives.

p.213

The key to motivation is motive.

p.112

Vision is the fundamental force that drives everything else in our lives.

p.116

Perhaps the most important legacy we can
leave is vision.

p.116

Balance isn't either/or; it's *and*.

p.118

February 21

Success in one role can't justify failure in another.

p.125

There's no way we can escape accountability. We *do* make a difference—one way or the other. We *are* responsible for the impact of our lives.

p.130

Time may be a limited resource, but we aren't.

p.134

You can want to do the right thing, and you can even want to do it for the right reasons. But if you don't apply the right principles, you can still hit a wall.

p.136

What do I desire to accomplish? What is the contribution I want to make? What is the end I have in mind? A principle-based "what" focuses on growth and contribution. It isn't just setting and achieving goals that creates quality of life. What we seek, we generally find. When we set goals that are in harmony with conscience and the principles that create quality of life, we seek—and find—the best.

p.141

The struggle comes when we sense a gap between the clock and the compass—when what we do doesn't contribute to what is most important in our lives.

p.19

Doing the right thing for the right reason in the right way is the key to quality of life.

p.144

To set and work toward any goal is an act of courage.

p.152

March 1

Priority is a function of context.

p.154

The perspective of the week prompts us to plan for renewal—a time for recreation and reflection—weekly and daily.

p.156

March 3

Without regular renewal, people are generally pushed in other directions. Instead of acting, they're constantly being acted upon.

p.157

March 4

Life is one indivisible whole.

p.160

March 5

Content in context empowers you to make more wise and effective decisions in your moments of choice.

p.164

March 6

Quality of life depends on what happens in
the space between stimulus and response.
p.167

March 7

Any week or day or moment in life is uncharted territory. It's never been lived before.

p.168

March 8

A moment of choice is a moment of truth.
p.169

March 9

We may find it convenient to live with the illusion that circumstances or other people are responsible for the quality of our lives, but the reality is that we are responsible— response-able—for our choices.

p.169

March 10

Over time, our choices become habits of the heart. And, more than any other factor, these habits of the heart affect our time and the quality of our lives.

p.170

The essence of principle-centered living is making the commitment to listen to and live by conscience.

p.170

Wisdom is a marriage—a synergy—of heart and mind.

p.175

Wisdom is learning all we can, but having the humility to realize that we don't know it all.

p.175

March 14

The key to acting with integrity is to simply stop playing the game.

p.178

March 15

It takes courage to realize that you are greater than your moods, greater than your thoughts, and that you can control your moods and thoughts.

p.178

Educating the heart is the critical comple-
ment to educating the mind.

p.180

Our body is a fundamental stewardship; it's the instrument through which we work to fulfill all other stewardships and responsibilities.

p.181

One of the best ways to educate our hearts is to look at our interaction with other people, because our relationships with others are fundamentally a reflection of our relationship with ourselves.

p.185

The value of any week is not limited to what we do in it; it's also in what we learn from it.*

p.189

---

* For complimentary samples of the weekly schedules from the 7 Habits Organizer, call 1-800-292-6839 or visit our Internet home page at www.covey.com.

It's important to be deeply honest and self-aware, to connect with conscience, to use independent will and creative imagination to consider possibilities and commit to positive change.

p.191

March 21

The shift is from doing more things in less time to doing first things in an effective, balanced, and synergistic way.

p.193

Our greatest joy—and our greatest pain—comes in our relationships with others. The fact is that quality of life is, by nature, interdependent.

p.197

March 23

The reality is that most great achievements were not made in a vacuum. The individual who receives the credit usually stands on the shoulders of many who went before.

p.197

The fact is that we're better together than
we are alone.

p.198

Humility comes as we realize that "no man is an island," that no one individual has all the talents, all the ideas, all the capacity to perform the functions of the whole.

p.198

Vital to quality of life is the ability to work together, learn from each other, and help each other grow.

p.198

To change the results, we need to change the paradigm.

p.200

Total quality begins with total personal quality. Organizational empowerment begins with individual empowerment.

p.202

Ultimately, there's no such thing as "organizational behavior"; it's all behavior of the people in the organization.

p.202

March 30

Trust is the glue of life.

p.203

March 31

Difference is the beginning of synergy.

p.211

April 1

Contrary to most of our scripting, "to win" does *not* mean somebody else has to lose.
p.212

April 2

The degree to which urgency drives the organization is the degree to which importance does not.

p.218

April 3

Frustration is essentially a function of expectation.

p.227

April 4

Win-win is not adversarial; it's synergistic.
It's not transactional; it's transformational.

p.235

April 5

We spend an incredibly inordinate amount of time dealing with symptoms of low trust, and *learning how to deal with the symptoms faster is not going to make a qualitative difference.*

p.237

April 6

We may not be *the* leader, but we're *a* leader.

p.239

April 7

Empowerment can't be installed; it has to be grown.

p.239

April 8

Character is what we are; competence is what we can do. The reality is that character and competence drive everything else in the organization.

p.240

Trust is the natural outgrowth of trust-worthiness. So the highest-leverage thing we can do to create trust is to be trust-worthy.

p.243

April 10

When structures and systems are aligned, they facilitate empowerment; when they aren't, they work against it.

p.244

April 11

Building character and competency is a process.

p.246

Because of its value, some people have called feedback "the breakfast of champions." But it isn't the breakfast; it's the lunch. Vision is the breakfast. Self-correction is the dinner. Without vision, we have no context for feedback; we're just responding to what someone else values or wants. We fall into the trap of trying to become all things to all people, meeting everybody's expectations, and we end up essentially meeting nobody's, including our own. But with a clear sense of vision and mission, we can use feedback to help us achieve a greater integrity.

p.247

The responses of others reflect not only how they see us, but also how well they feel we do those things that are important to them.

p.247

April 14

It takes humility to seek feedback. It takes wisdom to understand it, analyze it, and appropriately act on it.

p.251

April 15

Success is always inside out.

p.262

April 16

Assume good intentions. Your deeply held beliefs about someone will create the tone for any interactions you have.

p.262

April 17

We can never really change someone; people must change themselves.

p.262

April 18

If at first you don't succeed, *find out why.*

p.264

People are not truly self-governing unless they are free to fail.

p.264

Principle-centered living is not an end in itself; it's the means *and* the end. It's the quality of our travel along life's road. It's the power and peace we experience each day as we accomplish what matters most. In a principle-centered life, the journey and the destination are one.

p.267

April 21

Management works *in* the system; leadership works *on* the system.

p.268

April 22

It's not only a matter of when to do things,
but whether or not to do them at all.

p.270

April 23

We sometimes fail to think of our role in the family as a leadership role, but what an opportunity for impact! One of the greatest legacies we can leave our children is a sense of purpose and responsibility to correct principles.

p.275

We simply cannot be a law unto ourselves without consequence. Peace and quality of life come only as we discover and align with the fundamental Laws of Life.

p.280

April 25

Opposition is a natural part of life. Just as we develop our physical muscles through overcoming opposition (such as lifting weights), we develop our character muscles by overcoming challenges and adversity.

p.285

April 26

When our expectations aren't based on true-north realities, we set ourselves up for frustration and lack of peace.

p.286

Conscience is our connection to true north, to the principles that make peace and quality of life possible.

p.288

April 28

Two of the most deadly roadblocks to peace are discouragement and pride.

p.288

April 29

The best way to develop courage is to set a goal and achieve it, make a promise and keep it.

p.289

April 30

The antidote for the poison of pride is humility.

p.291

May 1

We are not laws unto ourselves, and the more we begin to value principles and people, the greater will be our peace.

p.291

Becoming principle-centered is just that: *becoming*. It's not arriving; it's a lifetime quest.

p.291

May 3

The important thing is to keep trying.

p.294

Every breakthrough is a break-with, a letting go. As we work to put first things first in our lives, it may be time for us to let go of things that are holding us back, keeping us from making the contribution we could make.

p.295

May 5

Life is learning—from our mistakes as well as our successes. "The only real mistake in life," said one, "is the mistake not learned from."

p.296

Each decision we make is an important decision.

p.296

We are absolutely convinced that the best way to create quality of life is to listen to and live by conscience.

p.302

Our two greatest gifts are time and the freedom to choose. The key is in not "spending" time, but in "investing" it.

p.302

May 9

Organization brings mental clarity and order.*

p.323

* For a complimentary four-week sample of the 7 Habits Organizer, call 1-800-292-6839 or visit our Internet home page at www.covey.com.

May 10

Personal responsibility is a valid and power-ful principle.

p.324

More than skill or technique, individual and organizational quality is a function of aligning both personal character and personal behavior with principles.

p.328

In our hands is the power to choose.

p.342

May 13

Instead of spending all our time just living, we can become aware of the consequences of our choices and learn from living.

p.343

The value of one choice over another is not always completely rational or easily defensible, but is discernible.

p.343

Living in harmony with nature is a vital part of quality of life.

p.343

Life is better when we treat others as we would be treated.

p.343

The great apparent dichotomy is that the more we give, the more we get.

p.343

For many of us, there's a gap between the compass and the clock—between what's deeply important to us and the way we spend our time.

p.16

May 19

We're constantly making choices about the way we spend our time, from the major seasons to the individual moments in our lives. We're also living with the consequences of those choices.

p.17

Putting first things first is an issue at the very heart of life.

p.18

What is "best" for you? What keeps you from giving those "best" things the time and energy you want to give them? Are too many "good" things getting in the way?

p.19

Our struggle to put first things first can be characterized by the contrast between two powerful tools that direct us: the clock and the compass. The clock represents our commitments, appointments, schedules, goals, activities—what we do with, and how we *manage* our time. The compass represents our vision, values, principles, mission, conscience, direction—what we feel is important and how we *lead* our lives.

p.19

May 23

In our effort to close the gap between the clock and the compass in our lives, many of us turn to the field of "time management."

p.21

May 24

Just because we value something does not necessarily mean it will create quality-of-life results. When what we value is in opposition to the natural laws that govern peace of mind and quality of life, we base our lives on illusion and set ourselves up for failure. We cannot be a law unto ourselves.

p.26

There's a vital difference between efficiency and effectiveness. You may be driving down the highway, enjoying great traveling weather, and getting terrific mileage. You may be very efficient. But if you're headed south down the California coast on Highway 101 and your destination is New York City—some three thousand miles to the east—you're not being very effective.

p.26

Most of the greatest achievements and the greatest joys in life come through relationships that are *transformational.*

p.27

Time management is essentially a set of competencies. The idea is that if you can develop certain competencies, you'll be able to create quality-of-life results. But personal effectiveness is a function of competence *and character.*

p.27

May 28

When structure and systems are aligned, they create integrity or integratedness. They facilitate rather than roadblock what you're trying to do.

p.245

May 29

More essential than working on attitudes and behaviors is examining the paradigms out of which those attitudes and behaviors flow.

p.30

May 30

As human beings, we're trying—sometimes with disastrous results—to run our businesses, raise our children, teach our students, be involved in relationships without giving serious and careful consideration to the roots out of which the fruits in our lives are growing.

p.30

People expect us to be busy, overworked. It's become a status symbol in our society— if we're busy, we're important; if we're not busy, we're almost embarrassed to admit it. Busyness is where we get our security; it's validating, popular, and pleasing. It's also a good excuse for not dealing with the first things in our lives.

p.35

June 1

Addiction to urgency is every bit as dangerous as other commonly recognized dependencies.

p.35

June 2

Many important things that contribute to our overall objectives and give richness and meaning to life don't tend to act upon us or press us.

p.36

Almost always, there *is* one thing among all others that should be done first.

p.40

June 4

The degree to which urgency is dominant
is the degree to which importance is not.

p.42

June 5

Simply doing more faster fails to get at the chronic causes, the underlying *reason* for the pain. It's doing nothing to really solve the chronic pain that comes from not putting first things first.

p.42

Quadrant II does not act on us; we must act on it. This is the Quadrant of personal leadership.

p.38

June 7

There are certain things that are fundamental to human fulfillment. If these basic needs aren't met, we feel empty, incomplete.

p.44

June 8

The key to the fire within is our need to leave a legacy.

p.49

Fundamental principles have been recognized—though sometimes by different names—in all major civilizations throughout time.

p.54

June 10

In the short run, we may be able to go for the "quick fix" with apparent success. We can make impressions, we can put on the charm. We can learn manipulation techniques—what lever to pull, what button to push to get the desired reaction. But long-term, the Law of the Farm governs in all areas of life. And there's no way to fake the harvest.

p.56

June 11

Vibrant health is based on natural princi-ples. It grows over time out of regular exer-cise, proper nutrition, adequate rest, a healthy mind-set, and avoiding substances that are harmful to the body.

p.57

June 12

Economic well-being is based on principles of thrift, industry, saving for future needs, and earning interest instead of paying it.

p.57

June 13

Quality relationships are built on principles—especially the principle of trust.

p.57

June 14

The greatest fulfillment in improving ourselves comes in our empowerment to more effectively reach out and help others.

p.58

June 15

There is no way quality of life can grow out of illusion. The quick fixes, platitudes, and personality-ethic techniques that violate basic principles will never bring quality-of-life results.

p.58

June 16

As human beings, we have unique endowments that distinguish us from the animal world. These endowments reside in that space between stimulus and response, between those things that happen to us and our response to them.

p.58

Self-awareness is our capacity to stand apart from ourselves and examine our thinking, our motives, our history, our scripts, our actions, and our habits and tendencies.

p.59

June 18

Conscience connects us with the wisdom of the ages and the wisdom of the heart.

p.60

June 19

While environment or genetic influences may be very powerful, they do not control us. We're not victims. We're not the product of our past.

p.60

June 20

Imagination without independent will can create an idealistic dreamer; imagination without conscience can create a Hitler.

p.61

Keeping a personal journal is a high-leverage Quadrant II activity that significantly increases self-awareness and enhances all the endowments and the synergy among them.

p.63

June 22

If you're not sure why you still do some things that you know are harmful or self-defeating, analyze it, process it, write it down. It builds awareness of your scripting. It helps you to make wise choices.

p.63

Dreaming builds creative imagination. Then test your dreams. Are they based on principles? Are you willing to pay the price to achieve them?

p.64

June 24

Develop your imagination—you can use it to create in your mind what you hope to create in your life.

p.64

June 25

Writing truly imprints the brain, helps you remember and apply the things you're trying to do.

p.64

June 26

The existence of conscience is one of the most widely validated concepts in psychological, sociological, religious, and philosophical literature throughout time.

p.65

June 27

If we stop and search deeply with an honest heart, we can tap into that inner wellspring of wisdom.

p.65

June 28

There is an independent universal reality outside ourselves that conscience affirms.

p.67

It actually takes even more discipline, sacrifice, and wisdom to develop an educated conscience than it does to become a great sculptor, golfer, surgeon, Braille reader, or concert pianist.

p.67

June 30

An educated conscience impacts every aspect of our lives.

p.67

July 1

It's not enough just to listen to conscience: we must also respond. When we fail to act in harmony with our inner voice, we begin to build a wall around the conscience that blocks its sensitivity and receptivity. As C. S. Lewis observed, "disobedience to conscience makes conscience blind."

p.68

July 2

True security doesn't come from the way people treat us or from comparing ourselves to others. It comes from our basic integrity.

p.68

When people really think win-win, when they seek to deeply understand each other, and they focus their energy toward solving problems synergistically instead of against each other, the effects are profound.

p.234

July 4

Out of private victories, public victories begin to come.

p.69

July 5

You have the power to look at your own involvement, to observe your response, to change it.

p.70

July 6

Principles are the simplicity on the far side of complexity.

p.71

July 7

The same principle of synergy that makes it possible for two boards to hold more weight together than the combined weight held by each separately also empowers two people to come up with a solution better than either could have alone.

p.71

July 8

Our security comes from our own integrity to true north.

p. 72

We come to the principle to be taught by it. And as we learn where we went wrong in accordance with that principle, we can turn weaknesses into strengths.

p. 72

July 10

Humility truly is the mother of all virtues. It makes us a vessel, a vehicle, an agent instead of "the source" or the principal. It unleashes all other learning, all growth and process.

p.72

July 11

We all have basic needs and capacities that
are fundamental to human fulfillment.

p.73

There's a sense of peace when we're out in nature. Seasons come and go with regularity. There are cycles of life, giving and receiving in a beautiful, harmonious whole. Even cataclysmic events—storms, earthquakes, floods—are part of a larger harmony, a natural cycle of growth and change. Nature is always becoming. The beauty of nature constantly unfolds in accordance with its laws. Nature teaches us much about peace. It reminds us that there are laws and that they are in control. With that reminder is a sense of comfort that there is order in the universe.

p.278

July 13

To be effective, a tool must be aligned with reality and enhance the development and use of that inner compass.

p.74

July 14

Create a flexible framework for effective decision making instead of a schedule made of cement.

p.76

July 15

Quadrant II organizing can empower you to live, to love, to learn, and to leave a great and enduring legacy.

p.76

If we learn to pause in the space between stimulus and response and consult our internal compass, we can face change squarely, confident that we're being true to principle and purpose, and that we're putting first things first in our lives.

p. 76

We have to water, cultivate, and weed on a regular basis if we're going to enjoy the harvest. The difference between our own active involvement as gardeners and neglect is the difference between a beautiful garden and a weed patch.

p.77

Whatever your current quality of life, the Quadrant II process will produce significant results.

p. 78

Develop your personal capacity to understand and align your life with the principles
that govern quality of life.

p. 78

July 20

It's important to make sure that whatever system you use is aligned with what you're trying to do.

p. 78

July 21

Daily planning provides us with a limited view. Weekly organizing, on the other hand, provides a broader context to what we do. The activities of the day begin to take on more appropriate dimensions when viewed in the context of the week.

p.79

July 22

The first step is to connect with what's most important in your life as a whole. Context gives meaning.

p.79

July 23

Connecting with your personal mission is foundational to operating out of the importance paradigm.

p.80

July 24

Consider: What difference would a clear vision of my principles, values, and ultimate objectives make in the way I spend my time?

p.82

July 25

How would I feel about my life if I knew what was ultimately important for me?

p.82

Would a written statement of my life's purpose be valuable to me? Would it affect the way I spend my time and energy?

p.82

How would a weekly reconnection to such a statement affect the things I choose to do during the week?

p.82

July 28

We live our lives in terms of roles—not in the sense of role-playing but in the sense of authentic parts we've chosen to fill.

p.82

July 29

Roles represent responsibilities, relation-ships, and areas of contribution.

p.82

July 30

Much of our pain in life comes from the sense that we're succeeding in one role at the expense of other, possibly even more important roles.

p.82

July 31

A clear set of roles provides a natural framework to create order and balance.

p.82

August 1

Balance among roles does not simply mean that you're spending time in each role, but that these roles work together for the accomplishment of your mission.

p.82

Identifying roles gives a sense of the wholeness of quality life—that life is more than just a job, or a family, or a particular relationship. It's all of these together.

p.84

August 3

If we fail to build our personal capacity, we quickly become "dulled" and worn out from imbalance.

p.85

August 4

By identifying your roles, you're not trying to break your life down and fit it into neat little boxes on a planning page. You're creating a variety of perspectives from which to examine your life to ensure balance and harmony.

p.85

August 5

Consult the wisdom of your heart as well as your mind.

p.86

August 6

Begin to use your compass instead of the clock. Listen to your conscience. Focus on importance rather than urgency.

p.86

The key is to consistently do whatever builds your strength and increases your capacity to live, to love, to learn, and to leave a legacy.

p.87

The Quadrant II process allows for flexibility and encourages you to use your compass in determining what's most important for you to do.

p.87

Effectively translating high-leverage Quadrant II goals into an action plan requires creating a framework for effective decision making through the week.

p.88

The key is not to prioritize your schedule, but to schedule your priorities.

p.88

August 11

Make specific appointments with yourself to work on goals, and treat an appointment with yourself as you'd treat an appointment with anybody else.

p. 90

August 12

It's important to realize that opportunity may not surface at a predictable time.

p.90

It pays to examine each activity carefully and determine which quadrant it's really in. It may *feel* urgent. Is it? Or does it just seem that way because someone or something else is creating pressure? Is it really important? Or has the feeling of urgency made it only *seem* important?

p.92

August 14

It's critical *not* to fill every moment of every day with time-sensitive appointments. Allow for flexibility.

p.93

August 15

The daily task is to keep first things first while navigating through the unexpected opportunities and challenges of the day.

p.94

August 16

Exercising integrity, or integratedness, means translating the mission to the moment with peace and confidence—whether putting first things first means carrying out your plan or creating conscience-directed change.

p.94

If the nature of the day is such that nothing else gets done, you still have the satisfaction of knowing you did the one thing that mattered most.

p.95

The key is your ability to discern between two activities and determine which is more important at the time.

p.100

Quadrant II organizing empowers you to look at the best use of your time through the paradigm of importance rather than urgency.

p.100

When the unexpected is less important than what you had planned, Quadrant II organizing gives you perspective and the power to keep on track. When the unexpected is more important, it empowers you to adapt and change with confidence, knowing that you're acting on the truly important and not just reacting to the urgent.

p.100

Unless we learn from living, how are we going to keep from doing the same things—making the same mistakes, struggling with the same problems—week after week?

p.100

August 22

As you begin to think more in terms of importance, you begin to see time differently.

p.102

Vision can become a motivating force so powerful that it, in effect, becomes the DNA of our lives.

p.105

The power of transcendent vision is greater
than the power of the scripting deep inside
the human personality, and it subordinates
it, submerges it, until the whole personality
is reorganized in the accomplishment of
that vision.

p.106

When people have a real sense of legacy, a sense of mattering, a sense of contribution, it seems to tap into the deepest part of their heart and soul. It brings out the best and subordinates the rest.

p.106

August 26

Petty things become unimportant when
people are impassioned about a purpose
higher than self.

p.106

August 27

Creating and integrating an empowering mission statement takes time and earnest investment. In order to do it, we have to get into and create an open connection with our deep inner life.

p.109

One of the most powerful uses of self-awareness is to become aware of conscience and how it works within us.

p.109

Conscience puts us in touch with both the unique and the universal. Only as we tap into our conscience can we discover our unique purpose and capacity for contribution.

p.109

August 30

What you alone can contribute, no one else
can contribute.

p.110

Only as we connect with our conscience can we create the fire within.

p.110

September 1

We can act instead of being acted upon.
p.112

September 2

Each person's personal vision is unique.

p.112

The foundational principles and the recognition of the four needs and capacities—to live, to love, to learn, to leave a legacy—are transcultural, transreligious, transnational, transracial.

p.112

September 4

It's impossible to translate the mission to the moment in our lives without weekly cultivation—pondering over it, memorizing it, writing it in our heart and in our mind, reviewing it, and using it as the basis for weekly organizing.

p.113

An empowering mission statement has to become a living document, part of our very nature, so that the criteria we've put into it are also in us, in the way we live our lives day by day.

p.114

September 6

With nurturing and continuing cultivation, the mission statement becomes the primary factor that influences every moment of choice.

p.116

September 7

Creating and integrating an empowering personal mission statement is one of the most important investments we can make.

p.116

September 8

Roles are parts of a highly interrelated whole, a living ecosystem in which each part impacts every other part.

p.121

September 9

The reality is that the same person who gets up, showers, and eats breakfast in the morning is also the person who interacts with clients at the office, makes presentations to the board, coaches the Little League team, cleans out the garage, and goes to church. Whatever we are we bring to every role in our life.

p.122

September 10

A principle such as proactivity—accepting personal responsibility for your own life—is just as empowering in dealing with a disgruntled spouse or a rebellious teenager as it is in dealing with an irate customer, a demanding boss, or a frustrated direct report.

p.122

September 11

Principles empower us with an abundance mentality. There's more of everything.

p.124

September 12

Success or failure in any role contributes to the quality of every other role and of life as a whole.

p.125

September 13

The balance of nature itself teaches us the principle of times and seasons. There are times in our lives when imbalance is balance.

p.126

September 14

The vital factor in any choice concerning
balance in our lives is a deep connection
with our inner voice of conscience.

p.127

September 15

Because we live in an environment inundated by human *doing* more than human *being,* it's easy to get caught up in imbalance to the point that it no longer reflects mission or principles.

p.127

September 16

Only as we keep an open communication with our deep inner life will we have the wisdom to make effective choices.

p.127

September 17

We're stewards over our time, our talents, our resources. Stewardship involves a sense of being accountable to someone or something higher than self.

p.129

A significant part of effectiveness is in the balance between developing and doing, between production (P) and increasing our production capability (PC).

p.131

There's no balance in life without balance in our inner life—without the synergy created when living, loving, learning, and leaving a legacy coalesce.

p.132

As we create synergy among the roles of our lives, there's more of us to put into the time we have.

p.134

Goal setting is obviously a powerful process. It's based on the same principle of focus that allows us to concentrate rays of diffused sunlight into a force powerful enough to start a fire. It's the manifestation of creative imagination and independent will. It's the practicality of "eating our elephants one bite at a time," of translating vision into achievable, actionable doing. It's a common denominator of successful individuals and organizations.

p 136

Building character strength is like building physical strength. When the test comes, if you don't have it, no cosmetics can disguise the fact that it just isn't there. You can't fake it. It takes strength to set a heroic goal, to work on chronic problems instead of going for the "quick fix," to stay with your commitments when the tide of popular opinion turns against you.

p.138

Conscience is powerful because it creates alignment between mission and principles and gives guidance in the moment of choice.

p.140

Goals that are connected to our inner life have the power of passion and principle. They're fueled by the fire within and based on true-north principles that create quality-of-life results.

p.140

If you want to build a trusting relationship,
be trustworthy.

p.143

September 26

Our integrity is the basis of our confidence
in ourselves and the confidence we inspire
in others.

p.145

Self-awareness involves deep personal honesty. It comes from asking and answering hard questions.

p.145

September 28

Self-awareness prompts us to start where we are—no illusions, no excuses—and helps us to set realistic goals.

p.145

September 29

Frustration in life comes as a result of un-
met expectations.

p.145

Self-awareness is ear to the voice of conscience.

p.145

October 1

We can't act with integrity without being open to change.

p.146

When we make and keep commitments, such as setting and achieving goals, we make deposits. We increase our confidence in our own trustworthiness, in our ability to make and keep commitments to ourselves and to others. A high balance in this account is a great source of strength and security.

p.137

October 3

A principle-based goal is the right thing, for the right reason, in the right way.

p.146

Through conscience, we connect with the passion of vision and mission and the power of principles.

p.146

October 5

Through creative imagination, we envision possibility and synergistic, creative ways to achieve it.

p.146

October 6

Through self-awareness, we set goals with realistic stretch and stay open to conscience-driven change.

p.146

Through independent will, we make pur-
poseful choice and carry it out—we have
the integrity to walk our talk.

p.146

October 8

What are the one or two most important
things I could do in this role this week that
would have the greatest positive impact?
p.149

October 9

An effective goal is in harmony with our inner imperatives.

p.149

October 10

We need to be sensitive to our inner voice of conscience.

p.149

October 11

When we exercise the courage to set and act on goals that are connected to principles and conscience, we tend to achieve positive results.

p.152

October 12

When we exercise courage in setting goals that are not deeply connected to principles and conscience, we often get undesirable results that lead to discouragement and cynicism.

p.152

The power of principle-based goal setting is the power of principles—the confidence that the goals we set will create quality-of-life results, that our ladders are leaning against the right walls.

p.152

While the objective of most daily planning approaches is to help us put first things first, the reality is that daily planning keeps us focused on doing urgent things first. The perspective is insufficient to accomplish the result.

p.154

October 15

The week represents a complete patch in
the fabric of life.

p.156

Renewal is not mindless, purposeless escape activity.

p.156

Personal leadership is cultivating the wisdom to recognize our need for renewal and to ensure that each week provides activities that are genuinely re-creational in nature.

p.157

October 18

There are an infinite number of ways we can create synergy in our lives.

p.159

The objective is not to cram as many activities as possible into our schedule or to try to do everything at once.

p.159

October 20

We often tend to build walls between work, family, and personal time. We act as if what we do in one area doesn't affect what we do in the others. Yet, we all know that these barriers are artificial.

p.160

October 21

Whole-parts-whole thinking empowers us to see relationships and create the connections that lead to growth, contribution, and fulfillment instead of fragmentation, discouragement, and self-focus. It becomes a subconscious way of thinking that empowers us to integrate our lives and weave elements together in a beautiful pattern.

p.161

Weekly organizing puts *content*—the activities of our lives—into the *context* of what's important in our lives.

p.161

Quadrant II organizing is not prioritizing what's on the schedule; it's scheduling priorities.

p.161

October 24

Much of our frustration and anxiety comes from the feeling of being unprepared. Many activities become urgent as a result of lack of proper preparation.

p.164

The successful experiences most of us would like to have in life are rarely an accident. They are almost always an achievement, the result of careful planning and thorough preparation.

p.164

If our idea of effective time management is to bulldoze our way through a list of scheduled appointments and "to do's," no matter what, we're setting ourselves up for almost inevitable frustration. The nature of most days will violate that expectation, in addition to which we'll miss some of the richest, most meaningful dimensions of living.

p.168

October 27

The purpose of Quadrant II organizing is to empower us to live with integrity in the moment of choice. Whatever detours may come up, whatever new roads may be built after the map is created, we can depend on our internal compass to keep us moving in the right direction.

p.168

This is the essence of principle-centered living. It's creating an open channel with that deep inner knowing and acting with integrity to it. It's having the character and competence to listen to and live by your conscience.

p.172

October 29

The essential purpose of the Quadrant II process is to increase the space between stimulus and response and our power to act in it with integrity.

p.172

October 30

We pause between stimulus and response to proactively choose a response that is deeply integrated with principles, needs, and capacities.

p.172

As we face the challenges of the day, we need to create a key question that will draw us immediately into the focus of listening to and living by conscience.

p.173

November 1

People are more important than schedules.
p.174

November 2

Involve people in the problem and work
out solutions together.

p.174

November 3

We exhaust ourselves far more from the tension and the consequences of internal disharmony—not doing what we feel we should—than from hard, unremitting work.

p.177

November 4

Many of what we call "time management" frustrations—feeling hassled, pressured, caught in dilemmas—are, at the core, problems of inner dissonance.

p.177

November 5

Look at every expression of conscience as an invitation to create greater alignment with the fundamental Laws of Life.

p.178

November 6

Some of the greatest acts of courage are in that instant between stimulus and response in our everyday decisions.

p.178

November 7

Listening to and living by conscience becomes the fundamental habit of the heart.

p.179

Educating the heart is the process of nurturing inner wisdom.

p.180

A personal mission statement becomes the DNA for every other decision we make.

p.180

November 10

Studies repeatedly show the powerful negative effects of fatigue and illness on effective decision making.

p.180

November 11

As we study civilizations throughout time, we see the consequences in the lives of individuals and societies that lived by true-north principles . . . and those that didn't.

p.181

November 12

An individual's life is part of a greater whole.

p.182

People who listen to and live by their conscience experience deep fulfillment—even in the midst of difficulties and challenges.

p.185

The amazing thing is that, with all the negative consequences of violating conscience, we sometimes make that choice.

p.186

November 15

We often get into ruts, on treadmills, caught up in patterns and habits that aren't useful. We don't stop to ask, *What can I learn from this week that will keep next week from essentially being a repeat of the same?*

p.188

Quality in almost every role involves a relationship with at least one other individual.

p.197

November 17

The world we live in is the legacy of those who have gone before us. The choices we make in it create a legacy for those who will follow.

p.198

Personal trustworthiness makes trust possible.

p.199

November 19

We're so busy consuming that we don't take care of our capacity to produce.

p.200

November 20

We're part of a vast, highly interrelated living ecology.

p.200

November 21

Trust is something you can't fake or quick-fix.

p.204

Trustworthiness creates flexibility and emotional reserve in relationships.

p.205

Obviously, the "things" paradigm is appropriate *when we're managing things*. But it's inappropriate—and ineffective—when we try to apply it to people. It's like trying to play tennis with a golf club—the tool isn't suited to the reality.

p.207

Much of what we do in traditional time management is efficiently hacking at the leaves instead of effectively working at the interdependent root.

p.207

November 25

Control is such an illusion.

p.208

November 26

Self-awareness empowers us to have *other awareness.*

p.209

November 27

If we know how to listen to our own heart, we can listen to the hearts of others.

p.209

November 28

Real listening shows respect.

p.214

The point is that you're working together on the problem instead of against each other through the problem.

p.230

When the problem is before you instead of between you, you avoid generating negative cycles that could take months or years to resolve, and this powerfully affects time and quality of life for everyone involved.

p.231

December 1

The spirit of true empathy is foundational
to effective synergy.

p.233

December 2

Both character and competence are necessary to inspire trust.

p.241

December 3

There is no such thing as organizational behavior; there is only behavior of individuals within the organization. An organization becomes trustworthy only as the individuals in the organization become trustworthy.

p.243

December 4

Discouragement is being lost in the woods without a compass or an accurate map. It's discovering that many of the maps people hand us lead us farther away from where we really want to go. Courage, on the other hand, comes as a result of knowing there are principles, of fulfilling our needs and capacities in a balanced way, of having clear vision, balance between roles, the ability to set and achieve meaningful goals, the perspective to transcend the urgency of the moment, the character and competence to act with integrity in the moment of choice, the abundance mentality to function effectively and synergistically in the interdependent reality. Courage comes from the heart, and being in touch with the heart creates hope.

p.289

December 5

Whatever your Circle of Influence, whatever the culture, you can work toward creating shared expectations and understanding.

p.243

December 6

Anytime we help create shared vision and strategy, we empower ourselves and others.

p.244

Win-win takes people where they are, not where you want them to be. So you can meet them where they are.

p.259

"Accomplishing tasks through people" is a different paradigm than "building people through the accomplishment of tasks." With one, you get things done. With the other, you get them done with far greater creativity, synergy, and effectiveness ... and in the process, you build the capacity to do more in the future as well.

p.256

Make sure your paradigms are true to principle.

p.262

You don't do anyone a favor by artificially creating a soft set of expectations.

p.262

December 11

Establishing excessive controls to protect against the problems of a few people will affect the performance of the entire organization.

p.264

December 12

There are so many reasons why errors may occur that you rarely gain anything by coming unglued when people make a mistake.

p.265

Your organization's culture is the one competitive advantage that cannot be duplicated.

p.265

When we start to look through a leadership instead of a management paradigm, we begin to see opportunities in places we never really thought of before.

p.274

December 15

Only by acting in harmony with correct principles, exercising patience, humility, and courage, and working with your Circle of Influence can you transform yourself and positively influence your organization. You can only create empowerment from the inside out.

p.266

December 16

As we exercise self-awareness and examine our paradigms, we discover that they are deeply ingrained. Change is not easy.

p.277

December 17

Peace is essentially a function of putting first things first.

p.281

There are principles. We do have conscience. And those two things make all the difference. They impact our thoughts and how we see everything around us.

p.281

The problem is that many of our expectations come from scripting, the personality ethic, or the social mirror instead of true north. They're flawed paradigms. They're not based on the fundamental Laws of Life.

p.284

December 20

If our expectation is that there will be challenge, then challenge does not create frustration.

p.285

December 21

Only as we focus more on contributing than consuming can we create the context that makes peace in all aspects of life possible. It's in leaving a legacy that we find meaning in living, loving, and learning.

p.287

December 22

Without conscience, there is no peace.

p.287

People scripted in competition create competitive rather than cooperative systems. People with a fundamental urgency paradigm create systems that grow out of it.

p.242

December 24

We can only free ourselves to work on first things first as we let go of other things and focus our time and effort on the most important.

p.295

One of the most liberating experiences in life is to make the commitment to simply respond to conscience. People who try it, even for a week, are literally amazed at the release and at how much time and energy they discover has been spent justifying action contrary to conscience.

p.296

December 26

It's our firm conviction that by developing the capacity to listen to conscience and plan and organize effectively to do first things first, we can all make many individual and combined contributions that are currently falling by the wayside.

p.303

December 27

There is so much we can do to render service, to make a difference in the world—no matter how large or small our Circle of Influence.

p.306

December 28

You may find you're living with sub-conscious dreams that are not in harmony with your values. You may dream of living the life of Indiana Jones, but you don't really value the idea of crawling through cobwebs and sleeping with scorpions. If you don't get your dreams out in the open and look at them in the cool light of day, you may spend years living with illusions and the subconscious feeling that you're some-how settling for second best.

p.315

December 29

If the basic paradigm is flawed or incomplete, no amount of effective application or implementation is going to bring optimum results.

p.322

What is remarkable about "wisdom literature" is that, to the degree that we find
patterns, consistencies, and themes, it represents the most validated database in all
human experience. To ignore it—not to
try to learn from it—would seem an absurd
disregard of resource.

p.343

Principle-centered living is not an end in itself. It's the mean *and* the end. It's the quality of our travel along life's road. It's the power and peace we experience each day as we accomplish what matters most.

p.267

Appendix

Learn the Time Management Matrix

Many important things that contribute to our overall objectives and give richness and meaning to life don't tend to act upon us or press us. Because they're not "urgent," they are the things that we must act upon.

In order to focus on the issues of urgency and importance more effectively, let's look at the Time Management Matrix below. As you can see it categorizes our activities into four quadrants. We spend time in one of these four ways:

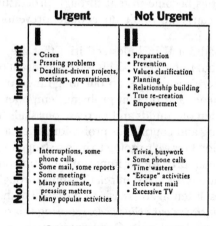

	Urgent	**Not Urgent**
Important	**I** • Crises • Pressing problems • Deadline-driven projects, meetings, preparations	**II** • Preparation • Prevention • Values clarification • Planning • Relationship building • True re-creation • Empowerment
Not Important	**III** • Interruptions, some phone calls • Some mail, some reports • Some meetings • Many proximate, pressing matters • Many popular activities	**IV** • Trivia, busywork • Some phone calls • Time wasters • "Escape" activities • Irrelevant mail • Excessive TV

© 1994 Covey Leadership Center, Inc.

Appendix

Quadrant I represents things that are both "urgent" and "important." Here's where we handle an irate client, meet a deadline, repair a broken-down machine, undergo heart surgery, or help a crying child who has been hurt. We need to spend time in Quadrant I. This is where we manage, where we produce, where we bring our experience and judgment to bear in responding to many needs and challenges. If we ignore it, we become buried alive. But we also need to realize that many important activities become urgent through procrastination, or because we don't do enough prevention and planning.

Quadrant II includes activities that are "important, but not urgent." This is the Quadrant of Quality. Here's where we do our long-range planning, anticipate and prevent problems, empower others, broaden our minds and increase our skills through reading and continuous professional development, envision how we're going to help a struggling son or daughter, prepare for important meetings and presentations, or invest in relationships through deep, honest listening. Increasing time spent in this quadrant *increases our ability to do.* Ignoring this quadrant feeds and enlarges Quadrant I, creating stress, burnout, and deeper crises for the person consumed by it. On the other hand, investing in this quadrant shrinks Quadrant I. Planning, preparation, and prevention keep many things from becoming urgent. Quadrant II does not act on us; we must act on it. This is the Quadrant of personal leadership.

Quadrant III is almost the phantom of Quadrant I. It includes things that are "urgent, but not important." This is the Quadrant of Deception. The noise of urgency creates the illusion of importance. But the actual activities, if they're important at all, are only important to someone else. Many phone calls, meetings, and drop-in visitors fall into this category. We spend a lot of time in Quadrant III meeting other people's priorities and expectations, thinking we're really in Quadrant I.

Quadrant IV is reserved for those activities that are "not urgent and not important." This is the Quadrant of Waste. Of course, we really shouldn't be there at all. But we get so battle-scarred from being tossed around in Quadrants I and III that we often "escape" to Quadrant IV for survival. What kinds of things are in Quadrant IV? Not necessarily recreational things, because recreation in the true sense of re-creation is a valuable Quadrant II activity. But reading addictive light novels, habitually watching "mindless" television shows, or gossiping around the water fountain at the office would qualify as Quadrant IV time wasters. Quadrant IV is not survival; it's deterioration. It may have an initial cotton candy feel, but we quickly find there's nothing there.

We'd like to suggest now that you look at the Time Management Matrix and think back over the past week of your life. If you were to place each of your last week's activities in one of these quadrants, where would you say you spent the majority of your time?

Think carefully as you consider Quadrants I and III. It's easy to think because something is urgent, it's important. A quick way to differentiate between these two quadrants is to ask yourself if the urgent activity contributed to an important objective. If not, it probably belongs in Quadrant III.

If you're like most of the people we work with, there's a good chance you spent the majority of your time in Quadrants I and III. And what's the cost? If urgency is driving you, what important things— maybe even "first things"—are not receiving your time and attention?

About the Authors

Stephen R. Covey is an internationally respected leadership authority and is founder and chairman of Covey Leadership Center. He is the author of *Principle-Centered Leadership* and *The 7 Habits of Highly Effective People*, which has sold over 10 million copies and has been translated into twenty-eight languages, and coauthor of *First Things First*.

A. Roger Merrill is vice president and a founding member of Covey Leadership Center. Roger is co-author of *First Things First,* author of *Connections— Quadrant II Time Management* and a contributing author to *Principle-Centered Leadership*.

Rebecca A. Merrill has served in numerous leadership positions in community, education, and women's organizations. Co-author of *First Things First* and *Connections—Quadrant II Time Management*, she also assisted Stephen R. Covey on *The 7 Habits of Highly Effective People* and *The 7 Habits of Highly Effective Families*.

About Covey Leadership Center

Stephen R. Covey is founder and chairman of Covey Leadership Center, an organization devoted to the development of principle-centered leadership based on many of the ideas described in this book. The mission statement of the organization reads:

> Our mission is to serve the worldwide community by empowering people and organizations to significantly increase their performance capability in order to achieve worthwhile purposes through understanding and living principle-centered leadership. In carrying out this mission, we continually strive to practice what we teach.

For more than a decade, Covey Leadership Center has been recognized as one of the world's premier leadership-development authorities, helping thousands of individuals and organizations solve personal, professional, and organizational problems through principle-centered leadership. Covey Leadership Center focuses on principles rooted in the unchanging natural laws that govern human and organizational effectiveness—laws that are timeless, universal, and intercultural.

This more than 700-member international firm is committed to empowering people and organizations to significantly increase their performance capability by building high-trust, high-performance cultures. Covey Leadership Center's client portfolio includes 82 of the Fortune 100 companies and two-thirds of the Fortune 500, as well as thousands of midsize and small companies, government entities, educational institutions, communities, families, and millions of individual consumers. The Center's work in principle-centered leadership is considered by its clients to be an instrumental foundation to the effectiveness of quality, leadership, service, team building, organizational alignment, and many other strategic corporate initiatives.

Its unique contextual approach to building high-trust cultures by addressing all four levels—personal, interpersonal, managerial, and organizational—is well renowned.

The firm empowers people and organizations to teach themselves and to become independent of the Center. To the adage by Lao Tzu, "Give a man a fish, you feed him for a day; teach him how to fish and you feed him for a lifetime," is added, "Develop teachers of fishermen and you lift all society." This empowerment process is carried out through programs conducted at facilities in the Rocky Mountains of Utah; through custom corporate on-site programs, consulting, and facilitator certification; and through public workshops offered in over 100 cities in North America and over 40 countries worldwide.

CLC products and programs provide a wide range of resources for individual, families, business, government, and nonprofit and educational organizations, including:

Programs

Covey Leadership Week
Principle-Centered Leadership
The 7 Habits of Highly Effective People
First Things First Time Management
The Power Principle
Facilitator Workshops for In-House Certification

Products

7 Habits Organizer time management system
Microsoft Schedule+ with 7 Habits Tools
7 Habits audio tapes
Living the 7 Habits audio tapes
Principle-Centered Leadership audio tapes
First Things First audio tapes
7 Habits of Highly Effective Families audio tapes
The Power Principle audio tapes
How to Write a Family Mission Statement audio tapes
7 Habits Effectiveness Profile

Stakeholder Information System (SIS) Baseline Report
Principle-Centered Living video
Covey Reference Library on CD-ROM
Covey Leadership Library video workshops
7 Habits poster series

Custom Consulting and Speeches

Custom Principle-Centered Leadership programs
Custom on-site programs
Consulting and speeches
Keynote addresses
Custom education programs

Publications

The 7 Habits Magazine
The 7 Habits of Highly Effective People
Principle-Centered Leadership
First Things First
First Things First Every Day
Daily Reflections of Highly Effective People
The Power Principle

Covey Leadership Center
3507 North University Avenue, Suite 100
Provo, Utah 84604-4479

Toll Free
1-800-292-6839
Fax
801-342-6236
International
801-229-1333 or by fax 801-229-1233
Internet: http://www.covey.com

Announcing the First Things First Time Management Workshop

This workshop provides an in-depth learning experience based on the acclaimed book *First Things First,* available as an in-house or public workshop. The First Things First Time Management workshops are taught to two-thirds of the Fortune 500 companies, thousands of small to mid-sized organizations, and government and educational institutions worldwide. Each participant will receive a **7 Habits Organizer**—the first breakthrough in time management in years—a First Things First audio tape, a hardbound edition of *First Things First,* and an implementation manual.

Send information to:

Name _____ Title _____
Organization _____
Address _____
_____
City _____ State _____ Zip _____
IMPORTANT! Phone Numbers(s): _____

Mail this coupon to:
Attn: Greg Link, Covey Leadership Center
P.O. Box 19008, Provo, UT 84605-9925

Or Call: 1-800-292-6839
Or Fax: 1-801-342-6236
Internet: http://www.covey.com

Please send me:

Registration and pricing information on the First Things First Time Management workshop in:

City Name: _____

❑ A free 7 Habits application workbook and sample organizer. Contains samples, weekly worksheets, mission statements, self profile, and win-win agreements.
❑ Information about Covey Leadership Center workshops:
  ❑ 7 Habits
  ❑ First Things First Time Management
  ❑ The Power Principle
  ❑ Principle-Centered Leadership
  ❑ Covey Leadership Week
❑ Information about the 7 Habits Organizer (available in four paper versions or the Microsoft Schedule+ with Seven Habits Tools electronic version).
❑ Information about custom speeches and keynote addresses
❑ Information about custom and video-facilitated programs that can be taught inside my company

Customer Information
Purchasing influence
  ❑ Decision-making
  ❑ Recommending
  ❑ None
Income: ❑ $0–$35,000 ❑ $35,001–$75,000 ❑ $75,001+